Cappuccino/Espresso
The Book of Beverages

Christie Katona
Thomas Katona

BRISTOL PUBLISHING ENTERPRISES
San Leandro, California

a nitty gritty® cookbook

ISBN 1-55867-212-5

Cover design: Frank J. Paredes
Cover photography: John A. Benson
Food styling: Susan Massey
Illustrations: Shanti Nelson

Contents

Espresso-Based Drinks: The Basics

In 1992 we wrote *The Coffee Book**, which is a collection of delicious food recipes that either use coffee or go well with coffee. While *The Coffee Book* includes several coffee drinks, our publisher could see a need for a book dedicated to solely to coffee drinks. When we started to do the research for this book, we discovered how true that was.

We found that published information on coffee drinks was scarce to the point of being almost nonexistent. As a result, we turned to those people who would be most knowledgeable about espresso and espresso drinks, the espresso stand owners and operators, and the suppliers who cater to them. The more interesting drink combinations inside this book are the result of the suggestions and recipes generously shared by those entrepreneurs, operators and business people. We also have to confess to some enthusiastic experimenting on our part.

We have what we think is a great collection of recipes that include espressos, cappuccinos, lattes, cold drinks for hot summer days, and spirited drinks for cold winter nights. We are glad we can bring these together in one book so you can enjoy them, too.

*pulished by Bristol Publishing Enterprises, Inc.

A Little History

By most accounts, the discovery of coffee took place around 600 AD. It is widely believed that Ethiopian tribesmen discovered the coffee plant growing in the wild while tending their herds. The tribesmen mixed the ground berries with animal fat and rolled the resulting mixture into balls for eating during their journeys. For the next 400 years, the berries were used primarily for food (although some resourceful person discovered the berries could be fermented into wine). The use and cultivation of the beans eventually migrated to Arabia where somewhere between the 10th and 15th centuries (the scholars are still arguing about when), the Arabs learned to steep the beans in water to make a delicious brew they called *qahwa*, which translates to something like "that which makes one able to do without something" (without sleep?). The brew, considered by some to be a potent medicine, was known for its restorative powers as well as being a delicious beverage. By the end of the 15th century, Arabian coffee houses were popular meeting places and coffee was an established part of Arabian life.

As early as the 13th century, Arabia was shipping coffee from Arabian ports including Mocha, which is the source of the name for this famous coffee bean. The enterprising Arabian merchants who grew and sold the beans shrewdly prevented any viable seeds and coffee plants from being exported, protecting their monopoly on the product. For several hundred years, they were successful at keeping the source of the beans to themselves and enjoyed a brisk trade and high profits.

However, it is hard to keep a good thing to oneself forever. In the 17th century it is reputed that a Moslem pilgrim was successful at smuggling a coffee plant and/or seeds home to his native India. From this humble start, the first coffee plantation in India was started at Kamatak and quickly spread to dozens of countries within a very short span of time. Dutch traders purchased some of the trees from the Kamatak plantation and began cultivating them in Java, which is the source of the *Mocha Java* coffee bean.

A young French naval officer, Captain Gabriel Mathieu de Clieu, is credited with being responsible for bringing the plant to the Caribbean via Martinique where it spread throughout the West Indies and eventually to Central and South America. The single coffee plant he brought to Martinique appears to be the progenitor of most of the billions of coffee plants that are now the major source of the world's coffee. The plant "acquired" by De Clieu was a descendent of a coffee plant given as a gift to Louis XIV. The king's coffee plants were cultivated in a hothouse at Louis XIV's Jardin des Plantes and were kept under close guard. De Clieu was able to obtain one of the plants through a romantic liaison with a lady of the court who had access to the hothouse; the rest is history.

Romance also played a part in the spread of coffee production to Brazil. There is evidence that Brazil clandestinely acquired the coffee plant through Dutch Guyana, where a Brazilian Army Lieutenant smuggled the plant back to Brazil with the aid of the wife of the local governor, who was enamored with the Lieutenant.

Coffee spread from Arabia first to Turkey and eventually to Europe. It appears that Venetian traders were responsible for introducing coffee to European markets. The first coffee house in England opened in 1637 and within three decades had spread throughout the country. English coffee houses became a center for social, intellectual, commercial and political discussions. These coffee houses became known as "penny universities," because by paying a penny admission price, you could hear intellectual discussions as well as the latest gossip and news while enjoying your cup of coffee.

In the American colonies, the Dutch had introduced English-style coffee houses. However, until the American revolution and the Boston Tea Party, tea was the preferred American beverage. Starting with the boycott of English tea, the beverage of choice in America became coffee and to date has remained the preferred beverage for most Americans.

About Espresso

Espresso is a strong, dark-roasted version of coffee that is brewed through a special steam-extraction process. Espresso originated in Italy, but it is now popular all over the world. Nearly all of the recipes in this book use espresso as the main ingredient.

In the past, most people associated the term espresso with a concentrated and bitter brew. However, there has been a new awareness of espresso and high quality coffees in general created within the last several years due to articles in magazines, newspapers and promotions by the coffee industry. As a result, the general public has become more sophisticated and discerning in their taste, and the old reputation for espresso has been replaced by an enthusiasm for espresso-based drinks as evidenced by the long lines at the espresso stands.

The term *espresso* is Italian for fast and primarily describes the method of preparation. The espresso brewing method uses pressure rather than gravity to rapidly extract the essence of the coffee in a concentrated form. Espresso is also used to describe the blend of beans and the degree of roast for the beans used to prepare espresso. Espresso roast is one of the darkest roasts and is characterized by a slightly burnt flavor.

Almost all coffee specialty shops now have commercial espresso machines and serve both espresso and espresso drinks to a growing number of enthusiasts. In the Seattle area, espresso has become something of a phenomenon. In addition to the specialty shops, curbside espresso carts and drive-through espresso windows have sprung up throughout the greater metropolitan area. Now, it seems that every shopping mall and supermarket has its own espresso station.

Automated espresso machines are also becoming common in cafeterias and at convenience stores in our area of the country. The best of these machines have digital readouts, offer choices in size, strength, type of drink, and even allow the addition of flavors. Although they cannot offer the range of choices offered by an espresso cart, we have been hard-pressed to taste a difference between hand-brewed and computer-brewed with some of the better machines.

At the beginning of the espresso rage, demand was greater than the supply. Then, the espresso shop/cart owner had a very lucrative business with more customers than he or she could handle. Not counting the investment, he or she was generally selling the drinks at 8 to 10 times the material costs for coffee, milk, flavorings, and cups and napkins. Now, with so many competitors, prices have dropped and operators are offering incentives to get customers to buy from their store or cart rather than from the competitor across the street. Our local grocery store provides a coupon for a free latte with the purchase of $50 or more of groceries. Many of the drive-through latte stands now offer punch cards that give you a free drink after you accumulate a certain number of punches. The best deal we have found so far is buy four and get the fifth for free with no limitation on the size. Isn't competition wonderful?

Espresso Bar Basics

You will find that there is an enormous variety of espresso-based drinks as well as flavored steamed milk drinks available at the espresso bars. Below is a list of the basics you should find at any modern espresso stand:

Espresso Macchiato   An espresso topped with a dollop of foamed milk

Espresso Con Panna   An espresso topped with a dollop of whipped cream

Espresso Ristretto   A short espresso (less than 1 ounce), accomplished by turning off the pump a few seconds earlier than normal

Espresso Doppio   A drink similar to ristretto, but with two shots of espresso served in a small cup

Espresso Romano   An espresso served with a lemon wedge or the zest of a lemon

Café Americano	Filtered hot water added to a shot of espresso
Cappuccino	An espresso topped with steamed and foamed milk. Its name is derived from the thick cap of foamed milk on top of the drink, which resembles the long, pointed cowl, or *cappuccino*, worn by Capuchin friars.
Wet Cappuccino	A cappuccino with approximately ⅓ espresso, ⅓ steamed milk and ⅓ foamed milk
Dry Cappuccino	A shot of espresso with the remainder of the cup filled with foamed milk
Café Latte	A shot of espresso added to steamed and foamed milk. It can also be called simply *latte*. Many flavors can be added to a latte for the nonpurist.
Latte Breve	A latte made with steamed half-and-half instead of milk
Latte Macchiato	A cup of frothed milk "marked" with a spot of espresso. Steamed milk is added to the cup first and is topped with foamed milk. Espresso is poured through the foam, which leaves the "mark."

Café Mocha	Espresso mixed with steamed milk and chocolate syrup. It can also be simply called mocha. It is usually topped with whipped cream and cocoa powder.
Steamer	Steamed milk mixed with flavored syrup. Almond, vanilla and hazelnut are popular flavors.

Sizes and Strengths

Every coffee house or stand has its own terminology for classifying espresso drinks. Following is a list of common terms used to describe the size and strengths of the drinks.

Sizes

Short/Regular: 8-ounce cup
Tall/Medium: 12-ounce cup

Grande/Large: 16-ounce cup
Venti/Extra-Large: 20-ounce cup

Strengths

Single: 1 shot of espresso
Double: 2 shots of espresso

Triple: 3 shots of espresso
Quad: 4 shots of espresso

Making Espresso at Home

There are many espresso machines intended for home use available in specialty stores. These range from less expensive "Moka" pots, which are heated on your stovetop, to very sophisticated pump-driven espresso machines. Prices for the automatic machines run from just under $100 to about $700, depending on the features and quality desired. Achilles Gaggia is credited with making the first modern espresso machine at the end of World War II. Gaggia's machine replaced steam pressure with a mechanical piston, which provided good control over the brewing pressure. All espresso machines work by forcing hot, pressurized water through finely ground espresso coffee that is packed tightly into a filter basket to make individual cups of espresso.

There are four variables to take into consideration when brewing the perfect cup of espresso: grind, quantity of grounds, tamp and rate of pour.

Grind: Espresso beans should be ground very finely. Ask the clerk where you purchase coffee beans or consult the instructions for your coffee grinder for specifics.

Quantity of grounds: Manufacturers differ, so consult the instruction manual for your machine to determine the correct amount of grounds to place in the filter basket.

Tamp: This refers to how tightly the ground espresso is packed into the filter basket. Consult the manufacturer's instructions for specific guidelines.

Rate of pour: This refers to how slow or fast the coffee drips from the filter basket. It will vary depending on the fineness of the coffee grounds and how tightly the coffee is tamped. Consult the manufacturer's instructions for specific guidelines.

These four variables have a greater influence on the final taste of the brewed espresso than they do on the taste of the drip-brewed coffee. You will have to experiment with the four variables since different brand machines have different operating pressures. Generally, the higher the operating pressure, the finer the grind of coffee you will use. Home machines usually operate in the area of 130 pounds per square inch (psi). The ideal water temperature is 193°F to 197°F, which may or may not be adjustable on your machine. Be sure to closely follow the manufacturer's instructions for your espresso machine.

The more sophisticated models of espresso machines from each manufacturer also provide a steaming nozzle that steams and foams milk for cappuccinos, lattes and steamers (see pages 15 to 17 for specific information on milk). Many of the recipes in this book make use of steamed and foamed milk. We recommend that you purchase an espresso machine that comes with this attachment, or use a special milk frother for this purpose (see page 17).

Brewing Essentials

Regardless of the equipment you choose to use, there are a few essential things to do in order to make good espresso at home:

1. **Start with good quality, freshly roasted espresso beans**. The importance of good-quality coffee beans is paramount. If you start with inferior beans, you can't expect to brew a great cup of espresso.

2. **Use clean equipment**. Coffee contains oils and other substances that get deposited on your equipment and can taint the flavor of the next cup if not removed.

3. **Use fresh water**. If you're lucky to have a clean, fresh-tasting water supply, then cool running tap water will make a great cup of espresso. If your water has minerals or other substances that alter its taste, consider using filtered water or bottled spring water. If using tap water, let the cold water run for a time to aerate it. Remember that your end product is still mostly water.

4. **Use the correct grind**. Ideally, you should grind your own beans just before making your espresso. Set your coffee grinder to the correct setting for espresso. Or, ask the sales clerk at the coffee store to grind your beans for an espresso machine; store unused beans in an airtight container.

5. **Use the right amount of coffee**. This is determined by the capacity of your machine and will affect the rate of pour. Generally, you will fill your filter insert almost completely, leaving just a little room for expansion of the grounds. Most home machines use about 1½ tablespoons of coffee grounds per cup. The rate of pour is best determined by experimenting. However, as a guideline, a single-shot machine should produce about 1 to 1¼ ounces of espresso in about 25 seconds.

6. **Use the correct water temperature**. This is automatic on the better machines.

7. **Serve espresso immediately after brewing**.

Beyond using good quality beans, fresh water and clean equipment, the secret to making good espresso is to avoid either under- or over-extracting the coffee essence. If the grind is too fine or the tamping too tight, the flow will be restricted, resulting in an over-extracted and bitter espresso. If the grind is too coarse or if the grounds are not tamped tightly enough, the water will flow too quickly, resulting in a thin and insipid espresso.

If your cup of espresso has a creamy golden froth on top after the pour, you have done a good job. The dense foam topping is called the *crema* and it is a sign that you have brewed a full-bodied and flavorful espresso.

About Milk

It takes a little bit of practice to steam and foam milk, but once you get the feel for it, it's easy to make good, frothy espresso drinks.

Milk for hot espresso drinks comes in two forms, steamed or foamed.

Steamed milk is milk that has been heated until very hot. It does not have much air incorporated into it, so it flows nicely when poured into the cup. Steamed milk is added to cappuccinos, mochas and lattes after the espresso has been added to the cup.

Foamed milk is steamed milk that has been infused with air until it is light and fluffy. Made properly, it should form a fairly dense "cap" when placed on top of the beverages. Foamed milk is spooned on top of the steamed milk in drinks such as cappuccinos and lattes.

There are two general ways to steam and foam milk for cappuccinos, lattes and mochas. The most common method is to use the steam nozzle that comes on the side of many good-quality espresso/cappuccino makers. The other method is relatively new to the marketplace, and uses a specialized piece of equipment specifically designed for frothing milk. These "milk frothers" were created to make the preparation of steamed and foamed milk easy to make and easy to clean up. Milk frothers resemble French press coffee pots, but have a special milk-foaming insert.

Frothing Milk with an Espresso/Cappuccino Machine

1. Use a clean, cold stainless steel pitcher. Using a steel pitcher will allow you to feel the milk's temperature as you heat the milk.

2. Fill the pitcher about 1/3 its capacity with fresh cold milk.

3. Following the manufacturer's directions for your espresso maker, open the steam valve briefly to bleed the steam nozzle of condensed water before steaming.

4. Insert the nozzle into the milk and open the steam valve fully.

5. Lower the pitcher until the nozzle is just below the surface of the milk and keep it there until sufficient foam is built for your purposes. For cappuccinos, let the foam rise to the top of the pitcher.

6. After the foam forms, lower the nozzle into the milk to continue the steaming process. The ideal temperature is about 150°F, which is about the point where the pitcher becomes too hot to hold for more than a second. If you want to be accurate, use a thermometer.

7. Turn off the steam and remove the pitcher from the nozzle. Let the pitcher of frothed milk settle for a few minutes. This gives you time to brew your espresso and let the foamed milk thicken a bit.

8. For cappuccino-style drinks, use a spoon to hold back the foam while pouring the steamed milk over the espresso. Then, spoon the thick foamed milk over the steamed milk and espresso to provide the foam cap for the cappuccino. The process is similar for lattes, steamers, breves, etc., except that less foam is used.

9. Clean the steaming nozzle thoroughly after each use.

If you want a lot of foam, use nonfat or low-fat milk. Whole milk and half-and-half will make richer drinks, but won't produce as much foam.

The lighter foamed milk will rise to the top of the frothing pitcher, while the heavier steamed milk will be found underneath.

Frothing Milk with a Milk Frother

1. Fill the carafe of the milk frother with cold nonfat milk to the level specified by the manufacturer.

2. Position the frothing lid on top of the carafe.

3. Move the wire mesh plunger up and down several times.

4. When the foam reaches the desired consistency, remove the lid.

5. Thoroughly wash the milk frother after each use.

Some manufacturers claim that the frothed milk can be heated in the microwave or on the stovetop. We didn't get good results during testing, but you can judge for yourself. Consult the manufacturer's instructions before attempting this and do not put any metal implements into the microwave.

Milk frothers can also be used to make whipped cream. Or, use cold, thick, foamed milk as a substitute for whipped cream when you are cutting down on fat and calories. Experiment by adding vanilla extract, flavored syrup or pureed fresh fruit.

About Flavorings

There are many flavored syrups on the market today, ranging from vanilla, chocolate and almond to strawberry, banana and kiwi. These syrups originated in Italy where they were used to flavor Italian sodas. The syrup-in-coffee craze started when the Torani Company brought its products to the United States in 1925. Now there are dozens of flavors on the market to use in coffee drinks, Italian-style sodas and other recipes. The syrups do not contain caffeine, are nonalcoholic and contain approximately 60 to 80 calories per ounce.

We find most of the fruit-flavored syrups are best in iced drinks and the nut, spice and richer flavors are more suited to lattes, cappuccinos and mochas. Somehow, the addition of chocolate to coffee rounds out the flavors and makes it more compatible with syrups such as orange, raspberry, strawberry, banana, coconut and mint.

A popular way to use flavored syrups is to make Italian cream sodas. Following is a basic recipe. Vary the flavorings to suit your taste. The fruit-flavored syrups are especially delicious for these.

Italian Cream Soda: Fill a 16-ounce glass with ice. Add 2 oz. flavored syrup and 1 oz. half-and-half and fill the glass with soda water. Stir with a tall spoon or straw to combine flavors. Top with whipped cream, if desired.

Flavored Syrups

It seems as if there is an endless supply of syrup flavors and the list changes almost daily. An amazing array of flavors can be found to make delicious combinations of espresso drinks and other beverages. The ideas are limited only by your imagination. If you can't find flavored syrups in your local specialty store or coffeehouse, the following companies can provide information.

Capriccio
818-718-7620

Da Vinci Gourmet
800-640-6779
http://www.davincigourmet.com

Entner-Stuart
800-377-9787

Forklore Foods
509-865-4772

Ghirardelli
800-877-9338

Guittard Chocolate Co.
800-468-2462

Monin, Inc.
800-966-5225
http://www.monin.com

Sergio Fine Flavoring Syrups
888-473-7446
http://www.syrups.com

Stirling Gourmet Foods
800-332-1714
http://www.stirling.net

Stearns and Lehman, Inc.
800-533-2722

Torani
800-775-1925
http://www.torani.com

About Garnishes

The appearance of all espresso drinks can be enhanced by using just the right cup, glass or mug. Adding an appropriate garnish gives the finished product eye appeal as well as additional flavor. Some manufacturers make interesting toppings, such as raspberry powder or granulated brown sugar. Rolled wafers, dainty cookies and miniature candy bars can also enhance the presentation of your special espresso drinks. Usually, wholesale purveyors carry these items next to the flavored syrups. Finely chopped nuts can be prepared in advance and frozen. Toasting them gives them extra flavor as well as crunch. Just a sprinkling of cocoa powder, cinnamon or nutmeg can add that special touch. Toasted coconut is easy to prepare and store. Whipped cream is enjoyed by everyone. Try flavored whipped cream for a special flair; several recipes follow on pages 22 to 26. Experiment with adding flavored syrups or liqueurs to make your drinks even more special.

To toast nuts: Heat oven to 325°. Place nuts on a baking sheet in a single layer and bake for about 10 minutes, turning with a spatula halfway through baking time. Watch nuts carefully so they do not burn. Cool before using.

To chop nuts: Place nuts on a large cutting board in a circle about the diameter of the length of a large knife blade. Rock knife blade from tip to handle in a circular pattern over nuts until evenly chopped. Or, place nuts in a food processor workbowl or blender container and pulse until evenly chopped. Take care not to overprocess nuts or they will become the consistency of butter.

To toast coconut: Heat oven to 325°. Place shredded coconut on a baking sheet, spreading thinly. Bake on the center rack of oven for about 10 minutes, stirring frequently, until golden brown. Watch coconut carefully so it doesn't burn.

To shave or grate chocolate: Chill a bar of semisweet baking chocolate until very cool. Rub bar over the surface of a box grater (the largest holes) to make small shavings of chocolate.

To make chocolate curls: Chill a bar of semisweet baking chocolate until very cool. With a vegetable peeler, shave chocolate into decorative curls. Use immediately.

To make lemon or orange twists: Wash lemon or orange with warm soapy water, rinse well and pat dry. Using a citrus stripper or vegetable peeler, run the tool over the surface of the fruit, removing just the colored part of the peel.

To make whipped cream: Pour cold heavy cream into a clean, chilled bowl and whip with a whisk or hand-held mixer until it begins to to thicken. Add granulated or confectioners' sugar to taste and continue to whip until soft peaks form.

Flavored Whipped Cream

Servings: 6-8

Any of the syrups can be used to flavor whipped cream.

1 cup heavy cream
2 tbs. flavored syrup

In a chilled bowl, whip cream until it begins to thicken. Add syrup. Continue beating until soft peaks form. Store covered in the refrigerator if not using immediately.

Galliano Whipped Cream

This is great on drinks that use a licorice-type flavoring, such as sambucca or anisette.

1 cup heavy cream
2 tbs. confectioners' sugar
1 tbs. Galliano liqueur

In a chilled bowl, whip cream until it begins to thicken. Add sugar and liqueur. Continue beating until soft peaks form. Store covered in the refrigerator if not using immediately.

Chocolate Whipped Cream

Use this as the crowning touch for many espresso drinks. If you're not using the whipped cream immediately, there is a stabilizing product on the market called "Whip It." Look for it at specialty gourmet stores. A small envelope will help whipped cream hold for hours.

1 cup heavy cream
2 tbs. confectioners' sugar
2 tbs. cocoa powder

In a chilled bowl, whip cream until it begins to thicken. Add sugar and cocoa. Continue whipping until soft peaks form. Store covered in the refrigerator if not using immediately.

Kahlua-Chocolate Whipped Cream

Servings: 6-8

*Here is a variation of **Chocolate Whipped Cream** for extra-special occasions.*

1 cup heavy cream
2 tbs. confectioners' sugar
2 tbs. cocoa powder
1 tbs. Kahlua liqueur

In a chilled bowl, whip cream until it begins to thicken. Add sugar, cocoa and Kahlua. Continue whipping until soft peaks form. Store covered in the refrigerator if not using immediately.

Orange Whipped Cream

This makes a delightful topping for espresso drinks. Kahlua, amaretto, frangelico or brandy can be used instead of the Grand Marnier.

1 cup heavy cream
2 tbs. confectioners' sugar
1 tbs. Grand Marnier liqueur

In a chilled bowl, whip cream until it begins to thicken. Add sugar and liqueur. Continue whipping until soft peaks form. Store covered in the refrigerator if not using immediately.

Basic Espresso Drinks

Classic Espresso

Espresso is traditionally served in a demitasse cup, a tiny coffee cup. Many Italians sweeten their espresso with a sugar cube and drink it quickly like an alcoholic shot. For a double, triple or even quadruple shot, repeat the process as needed. Many of today's high-quality espresso machines can brew two shots of espresso at a time. You can vary this method to suit your taste; see page 7 for ideas.

1 shot espresso

Following manufacturer's directions for your espresso machine, brew espresso directly into a serving cup. Serve immediately.

Espresso Macchiato

Macchiato (pronounced "mah-kee-AH-toh") means "marked." Here, a freshly brewed espresso is marked with a dollop of foamed milk.

1 shot espresso
foamed milk

Following manufacturer's directions for your espresso machine, brew espresso directly into a serving cup. With a small spoon, place a dollop of foamed milk on top of espresso. Serve immediately.

Espresso con Panna

Panna means cream in Italian.

1 shot espresso
whipped cream

Following manufacturer's directions for your espresso machine, brew espresso directly into a serving cup. With a small spoon, place a dollop of whipped cream on top of espresso. Serve immediately.

Espresso Romano

Drink your espresso as they do in Rome.

1 shot espresso
1 lemon, well washed

Following manufacturer's directions for your espresso machine, brew espresso directly into a serving cup. With a citrus stripper, cut a long strip from the colored part of the lemon peel (zest) and serve with espresso. Serve immediately.

Café Americano

This is the Italian way to serve American-style coffee.

1 shot espresso
hot water

Following manufacturer's directions for your espresso machine, brew espresso into a small pitcher or cup. Pour espresso into an 8-ounce cup. Fill cup with hot water and serve immediately.

Cappuccinos and Mochas

Basic Cappuccino

This basic recipe can be infinitely varied to suit your personal taste. See page 8 for some suggestions. Make a double cappuccino with 2 shots of espresso.

1 shot espresso
steamed and foamed milk

Pour espresso into an 8-ounce cup. With a spoon, hold back foamed milk and pour steamed milk into cup until almost full. Top steamed milk with a thick cap of foamed milk. Serve immediately.

Variation: Flavored Cappuccino

Add about 1 oz. flavored syrup to cup with espresso.

Basic Mocha

Servings: 1

The combination of chocolate and coffee is a perfect marriage. It can be the foundation for a wide array of special combinations.

1 shot espresso
1 oz. chocolate ice cream topping, chocolate syrup or chocolate fudge syrup
steamed milk
whipped cream, optional
cocoa powder for garnish, optional

In a 12-ounce cup, combine espresso and topping. Fill cup with steamed milk and top with whipped cream, if using. Sprinkle with cocoa powder if desired. Serve immediately.

Rocky Road Cappuccino

Servings: 1

An ice cream favorite in a steaming cup!

1 oz. chocolate ice cream topping, such as Hershey's,
   or chocolate or chocolate fudge syrup
1 oz. hazelnut, maple nut or golden pecan syrup
2 shots espresso
steamed and foamed milk
miniature marshmallows
cocoa powder for garnish

In a 12-ounce cup, combine topping, syrup and espresso. Fill cup with steamed milk and top with foamed milk. Add miniature marshmallows and sprinkle with cocoa. Serve immediately.

Macadamia Fudge Cappuccino

Servings: 1

Macadamia nuts are high in calories, but also high in nutrition. One sip of this drink and you feel justified whatever the case may be.

1 oz. chocolate fudge syrup
1 oz. macadamia nut syrup
2 shots espresso
steamed milk
whipped cream
cocoa powder for garnish

In a 12-ounce cup, combine syrups and espresso. Fill cup with steamed milk, top with whipped cream and sprinkle with cocoa powder. Serve immediately.

Island Mocha

Tasting coffee can be just like tasting wine. The three main components to consider are flavor, acidity and body.

1 oz. chocolate fudge syrup
1 oz. macadamia nut syrup
½ oz. coconut syrup
2 shots espresso
steamed milk
toasted coconut for garnish

In a 12-ounce cup, combine syrups and espresso. Fill cup with steamed milk and sprinkle with coconut. Serve immediately.

Caramel-Nut Mocha

A good worker on a coffee plantation can pick up to 200 pounds of ripe coffee "cherries" per day.

1 oz. chocolate syrup
1 oz. caramel syrup
1 oz. coconut syrup
½ oz. almond or hazelnut syrup
2 shots espresso
steamed and foamed milk or half-and-half
finely chopped almonds or hazelnuts for garnish

In a 12-ounce cup, combine syrups and espresso. Fill cup with steamed milk, top with foamed milk and sprinkle with nuts. Serve immediately.

German Chocolate Cappuccino

Caramel, pecans and coconut combined in a cup!

1 oz. chocolate syrup
1 oz. caramel syrup
1 oz. coconut syrup
½ oz. praline syrup
2 shots espresso
steamed and foamed half-and-half
shaved chocolate for garnish

In a 12-ounce cup, combine syrups and espresso. Fill cup with steamed half-and-half, top with foamed half-and-half and sprinkle with shaved chocolate. Serve immediately.

Amaretto Fudge Cappuccino

The most common error in brewing espresso is brewing too much coffee from the grounds.

1 oz. amaretto syrup
1 oz. chocolate fudge syrup
½ oz. almond syrup
2 shots espresso
steamed and foamed milk
Chocolate Whipped Cream, page 24

In a 12-ounce cup, combine syrups and espresso. Fill cup with steamed milk, top with foamed milk and top with *Chocolate Whipped Cream*. Serve immediately.

Amaretto Almond Cappuccino

As Mae West once said, "Too much of a good thing is wonderful."

1 oz. amaretto syrup
1 oz. almond syrup
2 shots espresso
steamed milk
whipped cream
finely chopped toasted almonds for garnish, optional

In a 12-ounce cup, combine syrups and espresso. Fill cup with steamed milk and top with whipped cream. Garnish with chopped almonds if desired. Serve immediately.

Kahlua Mousse Breve Cappuccino

Servings: 1

Try drinking your dessert from a cup for a change.

1 oz. chocolate syrup
1 oz. Kahlua syrup
2 shots espresso
steamed half-and-half
Chocolate Whipped Cream, page 24
chocolate curls for garnish

In a 12-ounce cup, combine syrups and espresso. Fill cup with steamed half-and-half and top with *Chocolate Whipped Cream*. Garnish with chocolate curls. Serve immediately.

Mexican Mocha Cappuccino

The ideal storage temperature for chocolate is 78°F. If stored at temperatures too high, a gray "bloom" forms on the chocolate. The bloom detracts from the appearance, but it is harmless — just the fat content coming to the surface. It is common in Mexico to add chocolate and cinnamon to coffee drinks.

1 oz. chocolate syrup
1 oz. Kahlua syrup
2 shots espresso
steamed and foamed milk
cinnamon for garnish
cinnamon stick for garnish

In a 12-ounce cup, combine syrups and espresso. Fill cup with steamed milk, top with foamed milk and sprinkle with cinnamon. Garnish with cinnamon stick. Serve immediately.

White Chocolate-Macadamia Cappuccino

White chocolate isn't chocolate at all, but a combination of cocoa butter, coloring and flavoring. Finely chop it in the food processor using the steel blade.

1 oz. white chocolate, finely chopped
1½ oz. macadamia nut syrup
2 shots espresso
steamed milk
whipped cream
vanilla powder for garnish

In a 12-ounce cup, combine white chocolate, syrup and espresso. Fill cup with steamed milk, top with whipped cream and sprinkle with vanilla powder. Serve immediately.

La Dolce Vita

Ah, the sweet life — Italians enjoy flavoring their coffee drinks with licorice-flavored liqueurs.

1½ oz. anisette or sambucca syrup
2 shots espresso
steamed and foamed milk
lemon twist for garnish

In a 12-ounce cup, combine syrup and espresso. Fill cup with steamed milk, top with foamed milk and garnish with lemon twist. Serve immediately.

Piña Colada Cappuccino

Chocolate comes from an evergreen tree of the genus "Teobroma," meaning food of the gods.

1 oz. chocolate syrup
1 oz. coconut syrup
½ oz. pineapple syrup
2 shots espresso
steamed and foamed milk

In a 12-ounce cup, combine syrups and espresso. Fill cup with steamed milk and top with foamed milk. Serve immediately.

Banana Split Cappuccino

The coffee tree is actually a tropical evergreen shrub. Each shrub lives for about 15 years and produces enough beans annually to make 1 pound of ground coffee.

1 oz. chocolate fudge syrup
1 oz. strawberry syrup
½ oz. banana syrup
2 shots espresso
steamed milk
whipped cream
maraschino cherry for garnish
finely chopped nuts for garnish

In a 12-ounce cup, combine syrups and espresso. Fill cup with steamed milk and top with whipped cream. Garnish with cherry and sprinkle with nuts. Serve immediately.

Black Forest Cappuccino

The tangy Bing cherries, rich chocolate and a bit of orange and cinnamon make this a wonderful combination.

1 oz. chocolate syrup
1 oz. Bing cherry syrup
½ oz. grand orange syrup
2 shots espresso
steamed and foamed milk
freshly grated orange peel (zest) for garnish
cinnamon for garnish

In a 12-ounce cup, combine syrups and espresso. Fill cup with steamed milk and top with foamed milk. Sprinkle with orange peel and dust with cinnamon. Serve immediately.

Cherry Amaretto Mocha

On the back of a sweatshirt one day we saw the following Singles Ad: "Single Americano seeks companionship and possible ??! for winter commutes and café encounters. Enjoys long sips along beach. Feels at home in a paper cup, but loves to dress up in a ceramic cup and saucer. Seeking double tall latte, any flavor, who loves to go foamy and lidless. No decaf!! Refillable?! Maybe you can fill my cup...Photo appreciated. P.O. Box 993."

1 oz. chocolate syrup	2 shots espresso
1 oz. cherry syrup	steamed and foamed milk
1 oz. amaretto syrup	vanilla powder for garnish

In a 12-ounce cup, combine syrups and espresso. Fill cup with steamed milk, top with foamed milk and sprinkle with vanilla powder. Serve immediately.

Caramel Apple Cappuccino

This is just like eating a caramel apple, but without the stick!

1 oz. apple syrup
1 oz. caramel syrup
½ oz. vanilla syrup
2 shots espresso
steamed milk
whipped cream
vanilla powder for garnish

In a 12-ounce cup, combine syrups and espresso. Fill cup with steamed milk and top with whipped cream. Dust with vanilla powder. Serve immediately.

Apple-Cinnamon Cappuccino

Experts say that if your cappuccino foam is "dry" you should be able to stand a iced tea spoon in a 12-ounce cup and it won't fall over.

2 oz. apple syrup
½ oz. cinnamon syrup
2 shots espresso
steamed and foamed milk
cinnamon for garnish

In a 12-ounce cup, combine syrups and espresso. Fill cup with steamed milk, top with foamed milk and sprinkle with cinnamon. Serve immediately.

Raspberry Torte Cappuccino

Fresh raspberry season is all too short, so enjoy them anytime in this delicious drink.

1 oz. raspberry syrup
½ oz. crème de cacao syrup
2 shots espresso
steamed and foamed milk

In a 12-ounce cup, combine syrups and espresso. Fill cup with steamed milk and top with foamed milk. Serve immediately.

Raspberry Torte Breve Cappuccino

This drink is rich, warm and wonderful.

1 oz. chocolate syrup
1 oz. raspberry syrup
1 oz. crème de cacao syrup
1 shot espresso
steamed and foamed half-and-half

In a 12-ounce cup, combine syrups and espresso. Fill cup with steamed half-and-half and top with foamed half-and-half. Serve immediately.

Rich Raspberry Mocha

There's a surprise layer of chocolate that waits for you at the bottom of this delicious drink.

chocolate ice cream topping
1 oz. raspberry syrup
½ oz. crème de cacao syrup or crème de cacao liqueur
2 shots espresso
steamed and foamed half-and-half
chocolate curls and/or fresh raspberries for garnish

Coat the bottom of a 12-ounce cup with ice cream topping to taste. Add syrups and espresso. Fill cup with steamed half-and-half and top with foamed half-and-half. Garnish with chocolate curls and/or raspberries. Serve immediately.

Tangerine Raspberry Cappuccino

There is a tangerine-flavored liqueur on the market called Mandarin Napoleon, which can be used instead of the Mandarin orange syrup if desired.

1 oz. chocolate syrup
1 oz. Mandarin orange syrup
½ oz. raspberry syrup
2 shots espresso
steamed milk
Orange Whipped Cream, page 26
orange twist for garnish

In a 12-ounce cup, combine syrups and espresso. Fill cup with steamed milk and top with whipped cream. Garnish with orange twist. Serve immediately.

Strawberry Amaretto Mocha

Servings: 1

When Christie studied at Le Cordon Bleu in London, one of the culinary tricks she learned was to add a tiny bit of finely ground pepper to crushed strawberries to bring out the flavor. It sounds crazy, but try it sometime! However, we do not advise adding pepper to a cappuccino!

1 oz. chocolate syrup
1 oz. strawberry syrup
1 oz. amaretto syrup
2 shots espresso
steamed and foamed milk
vanilla powder for garnish

In a 12-ounce cup, combine syrups and espresso. Fill cup with steamed milk, top with foamed milk and sprinkle with vanilla powder. Serve immediately.

Lattes and Iced Lattes

Basic Latte

The amount of milk used in a latte is a personal choice. Play with the ratio of espresso to milk until it suits your taste. Make a double latte with 2 shots of espresso and use a larger cup. If desired, you can top off the drink with a small dollop of foamed milk.

1 shot espresso
steamed milk

Pour espresso into an 8- to 12-ounce cup. Fill cup with steamed milk. Serve immediately.

Variation: Flavored Latte

Add about 1 oz. flavored syrup to cup with espresso.

Crème de la Cream Latte

Servings: 1

This latte is truly a cut above the ordinary.

1 oz. crème de cacao syrup
1 oz. Irish cream syrup
1 shot espresso
steamed milk
whipped cream
vanilla powder for garnish

In an 8-ounce cup, combine syrups and espresso. Fill cup with steamed milk, top with whipped cream and garnish with vanilla powder. Serve immediately.

Irish Nut Latte

Servings: 1

If your milk is steamed too hot, flavored lattes may curdle. Be sure to keep the temperature just below 150°F.

1 oz. Irish cream syrup
1 oz. hazelnut syrup
1 shot espresso
steamed and foamed milk

In an 8-ounce cup, combine syrups and espresso. Fill cup with steamed milk and top with a small dollop of foamed milk. Serve immediately.

Honey Nut Latte

Servings: 1

Honey makes a wonderful sweetener for lattes.

1 tsp. honey
½ oz. hazelnut syrup
1 shot espresso
steamed and foamed milk
cinnamon for garnish

In an 8-ounce cup, combine honey, syrup and espresso. Fill cup with steamed milk, top with a small dollop of foamed milk and sprinkle with cinnamon. Serve immediately.

Caramel Nut Latte

Beethoven was said to be so fussy about his coffee that he counted the individual beans — 60 per cup!

½ oz. caramel ice cream topping
¾ oz. chocolate ice cream topping
½ oz. hazelnut syrup
1 shot espresso
steamed milk
whipped cream, optional
finely chopped peanuts, optional

In an 8-ounce cup, combine toppings, syrup and espresso. Fill cup with steamed milk and top with a small dollop of foamed milk. Top with whipped cream and peanuts if desired. Serve immediately.

Breve-Style Hungarian Hazelnut Latte

Servings: 1

This is a taste of old Vienna. Be sure to garnish with whipped cream and worry about the calories tomorrow!

1 oz. hazelnut syrup
½ oz. vanilla syrup
1 shot espresso
steamed half-and-half
whipped cream
shaved chocolate for garnish

In an 8-ounce cup, combine syrups and espresso. Fill cup with steamed half-and-half, top with whipped cream and garnish with shaved chocolate. Serve immediately.

Breve-Style Rum Praline Latte

This tastes like pecan pie with whipped cream in a cup.

1 oz. rum syrup
1 oz. praline syrup
½ oz. hazelnut syrup
1 shot espresso
steamed half-and-half
whipped cream

In an 8-ounce cup, combine syrups and espresso. Fill cup with steamed half-and-half and top with whipped cream. Serve immediately.

Baklava Latte

All the flavors of the rich Middle Eastern dessert are here in a latte.

1 oz. praline syrup
½ oz. hazelnut syrup
½ oz. maple walnut syrup
dash lemon syrup
2 tsp. honey
1 shot espresso
steamed and foamed milk
cinnamon for garnish
cinnamon stick for garnish

In a 10-ounce cup, combine syrups, honey and espresso. Fill cup with steamed milk, top with a small dollop of foamed milk, sprinkle generously with cinnamon and garnish with a cinnamon stick. Serve immediately.

Toffee Coffee Latte

Servings: 1

In 16th-century Constantinople, failure to provide your wife with coffee was "grounds" for divorce!

1 oz. caramel syrup
½ oz. praline syrup
1 oz. chocolate syrup
1 shot espresso
steamed and foamed milk
finely chopped toffee candy for garnish, optional

In an 8-ounce cup, combine syrups and espresso. Fill cup with steamed milk, top with a small dollop of foamed milk and garnish with toffee, if desired. Serve immediately.

Coconut Latte

You can use canned coconut cream instead of coconut syrup to make this drink.

1 oz. chocolate syrup
½ oz. coconut syrup
1 shot espresso
steamed and foamed milk
toasted coconut for garnish, optional

In an 8-ounce cup, combine syrups and espresso. Fill cup with steamed milk and top with a small dollop of foamed milk. Garnish with toasted coconut if desired. Serve immediately.

Coconut-Mocha Latte

Servings: 1

To some, the ritual of making the morning's first cup of coffee is as important as brushing one's teeth!

1 oz. chocolate ice cream topping or chocolate fudge syrup
½ oz. Kahlua syrup
1 shot espresso
steamed and foamed milk
chocolate-covered coffee beans for garnish, optional

In an 8-ounce cup, combine topping, syrup and espresso. Fill cup with steamed milk and top with a small dollop of foamed milk. Garnish with chocolate coffee beans if desired. Serve immediately.

Coconut Almond Latte

Servings: 1

The composer Bach liked coffee so much he named a piece "The Coffee Cantata."

1 oz. almond syrup
½ oz. coconut syrup
1 oz. chocolate ice cream topping
1 shot espresso
steamed and foamed milk

In an 8-ounce cup, combine syrups, chocolate topping and espresso. Fill cup with steamed milk and top with a small dollop of foamed milk. Serve immediately.

Cherry Almond Latte

History says that Napoleon drank seven pots of coffee a day.

1 oz. chocolate topping
½ oz. cherry syrup
½ oz. almond syrup
1 shot espresso
steamed and foamed milk

In an 8-ounce cup, combine topping, syrups and espresso. Fill cup with steamed milk and top with a small dollop of foamed milk. Serve immediately.

Variation: Cherry Vanilla Latte

Substitute vanilla syrup for almond syrup.

Breve-Style Hot Buttered Rum Latte

Servings: 1

If your espresso is too slow extracting (it should only take about 20 seconds), make sure the coffee is not ground too finely, tamped too lightly or you don't have too much in the basket.

1 oz. Swedish rum syrup
½ oz. vanilla syrup
1 shot espresso
steamed and foamed half-and-half
nutmeg for garnish

In an 8-ounce cup, combine syrups and espresso. Fill cup with steamed half-and-half, top with a small dollop of foamed half-and-half and sprinkle with nutmeg. Serve immediately.

Almond Butterscotch Latte

Servings: 1

When Marilyn Monroe married Arthur Miller in 1956, she used coffee to dye her white veil to match her beige dress.

½ oz. butterscotch ice cream topping
½ oz. chocolate topping
½ oz. almond syrup
1 shot espresso
steamed and foamed milk

In an 8-ounce cup, combine toppings, syrup and espresso. Fill cup with steamed milk and top with a small dollop of foamed milk. Serve immediately.

Chocolate Butterscotch Latte

Servings: 1

One shop in Seattle features beautiful enameled earrings with various espresso designs on them. Seattle takes its coffee seriously!

½ oz. butterscotch ice cream topping
½ oz. chocolate syrup
1 shot espresso
steamed and foamed milk

In an 8-ounce cup, combine ice cream topping, syrup and espresso. Fill cup with steamed milk and top with a small dollop of foamed milk. Serve immediately.

Fudge Brownie Latte

Servings: 1

If your latte has an "off," "green" or bitter flavor, check to make sure your beans aren't old or you haven't overextracted the grounds.

1 oz. chocolate fudge syrup
½ oz. vanilla syrup
½ oz. maple nut syrup
1 shot espresso
steamed and foamed milk
cocoa powder for garnish

In an 8-ounce cup, combine syrups and espresso. Fill cup with steamed milk, top with a small dollop of foamed milk and sprinkle with cocoa powder. Serve immediately.

Brownie-Nut Latte

Take care not to boil your coffee when brewing it, as it damages the flavor. Boiling vaporizes the coffee essence and extracts its bitter-tasting compounds.

1 oz. chocolate fudge syrup
½ oz. vanilla syrup
½ oz. macadamia nut or hazelnut syrup
1 shot espresso
steamed and foamed milk
finely chopped nuts for garnish

In an 8-ounce cup, combine syrups and espresso. Fill cup with steamed milk, top with a small dollop of foamed milk and sprinkle with nuts. Serve immediately.

Rich Chocolate-Nut Latte

Servings: 1

After all is said and done, the most important ingredients for a good cup of espresso are: pure water, high-quality beans and careful brewing.

1 oz. Irish cream syrup
1 oz. macadamia nut, hazelnut or praline syrup
1 oz. chocolate ice cream topping
1 shot espresso
steamed and foamed half-and-half

In an 8-ounce cup, combine syrups, topping and espresso. Fill cup with steamed half-and-half and top with a small dollop of foamed half-and-half. Serve immediately.

Chocolate Malt Latte

Servings: 1

Use the powdered malted milk mix from your grocery store for this drink. It's usually available near the cocoa mix.

3 tsp. powdered malted milk mix, plus more for garnish
1 oz. chocolate ice cream topping
1 shot espresso
steamed and foamed milk
cocoa powder for garnish

In an 8-ounce cup, combine malt powder, topping and espresso. Fill cup with steamed milk, top with a small dollop of foamed milk and sprinkle with cocoa powder and malted milk mix. Serve immediately.

Mandarin Chocolate Latte

Chocolate, orange and coffee make a wonderful combination. Always add the toppings and syrups to the cup first; some syrups, such as hazelnut and vanilla, may curdle if added later. This recipe lends itself to numerous variations. For example, substitute chocolate fudge syrup for chocolate topping; substitute orange syrup, grand orange syrup or Grand Marnier liqueur for Mandarin orange syrup; substitute an orange slice or twist for the chocolate sprinkles garnish.

1 oz. chocolate topping
1 oz. Mandarin orange syrup
1 shot espresso
steamed milk

Orange Whipped Cream, page 26, optional
chocolate sprinkles for garnish

In an 8-ounce cup, combine topping, syrup and espresso. Fill cup with steamed milk, top with *Orange Whipped Cream*, if desired, and garnish with chocolate sprinkles. Serve immediately.

Tropical Delight Latte

Flavors from the islands combine in this latte.

1 oz. Swedish rum syrup
½ oz. coconut syrup
½ oz. macadamia nut syrup
1 shot espresso
steamed and foamed milk

In an 8-ounce cup, combine syrups and espresso. Fill with steamed milk and top with a small dollop of foamed milk. Serve immediately.

E.T.'s Favorite Latte

Servings: 1

In Steven Spielberg's movie E.T., the little space creature enjoyed Reese's Pieces chocolate-peanut butter candies. Chocolate peanut butter syrup makes a great latte. While experimenting for this book, we did try adding peanut butter to a latte — we did not care for it, but others might.

1 oz. chocolate peanut butter syrup
½ oz. chocolate ice cream topping
1 shot espresso
steamed and foamed milk

In an 8-ounce cup, combine syrup, topping and espresso. Fill cup with steamed milk and top with a small dollop of foamed milk. Serve immediately.

PB&J Latte

Remember your favorite childhood sandwich? Now, drink the flavors with your grown-up coffee.

1 oz. chocolate peanut butter syrup
½ oz. strawberry, cherry or grape syrup
1 shot espresso
steamed and foamed milk

In an 8-ounce cup, combine syrups and espresso. Fill cup with steamed milk and top with a small dollop of foamed milk. Serve immediately.

Peanut Butter and Banana Latte

Servings: 1

The flavors from another favorite childhood sandwich make a tasty drink when combined with espresso.

1 oz. chocolate peanut butter syrup
½ oz. chocolate ice cream topping
½ oz. banana syrup
1 shot espresso
steamed and foamed milk

In an 8-ounce cup, combine syrup, topping and espresso. Fill cup with steamed milk and top with a small dollop of foamed milk. Serve immediately.

Banana Fudge Latte

Servings: 1

According to one espresso stand operator, she has a customer who regularly drinks SIX shots of espresso at a time!

1 oz. banana syrup
1 oz. chocolate fudge syrup
½ oz. vanilla syrup
2 shots espresso
steamed milk
Chocolate Whipped Cream, page 24
chocolate sprinkles for garnish

In a 10-ounce cup, combine syrups and espresso. Fill cup with steamed milk, top with *Chocolate Whipped Cream* and garnish with sprinkles. Serve immediately.

Banana Nut Latte

Coffee beans grown at low altitude are referred to as "soft," whereas coffee beans grown at higher altitudes are called "hard."

1 oz. banana syrup
1 oz. chocolate fudge syrup
½ oz. macadamia nut or hazelnut syrup
2 shots espresso
steamed milk
whipped cream
finely chopped nuts for garnish

In a 10-ounce cup, combine syrups and espresso. Fill cup with steamed milk, top with whipped cream and sprinkle with nuts. Serve immediately.

Mint Patty Latte

If you are using glass coffee mugs, place a spoon in the mug before pouring the hot coffee to prevent breakage.

1 oz. chocolate fudge or chocolate mint syrup, or chocolate ice cream topping
1 oz. peppermint or crème de menthe syrup
1 shot espresso
steamed and foamed milk
Peppermint Patty candy wedge for garnish, optional

In an 8-ounce cup, combine syrups and espresso. Fill cup with steamed milk and top with a small dollop of foamed milk. Place candy wedge on edge of cup, if desired. Serve immediately.

Apple Pie Latte

Old-fashioned goodness in a cup!

1 oz. apple syrup
dash cinnamon syrup
1 shot espresso
steamed and foamed milk
cinnamon for garnish

In an 8-ounce cup, combine syrups and espresso. Fill cup with steamed milk, top with a small dollop of foamed milk and sprinkle with cinnamon. Serve immediately.

Acapulco Mocha Iced Latte

Servings: 1

You can use either coconut cream or coconut syrup to flavor this drink.

ice
1 shot espresso
1 oz. chocolate syrup
1 oz. orange syrup or grand orange syrup
1 oz. coconut cream or coconut syrup
cold milk

Fill a 12-ounce glass with ice, add espresso and syrups and fill with cold milk. Stir to combine flavors and serve immediately.

Maple Nut Iced Mocha Latte

Servings: 1

This is rich and satisfying and is a quick pick-me-up drink.

ice
1 shot espresso
2 oz. maple nut syrup
1 oz. chocolate syrup
cold milk

Fill a 12-ounce glass with ice, add espresso and syrups and fill with cold milk. Stir to combine flavors and serve immediately.

Mocha Nut Iced Latte

This bittersweet latte is intensely flavored, but goes down cool.

ice
1 shot espresso
2 oz. hazelnut, golden pecan or macadamia nut syrup
1 oz. chocolate syrup
cold milk

Fill a 12-ounce glass with ice, add espresso and syrups and fill with cold milk. Stir to combine flavors and serve immediately.

Iced Mocha Mint Latte

Servings: 1

Fresh mint is so easy to grow in your garden or in a planter. Use a sprig to garnish this refreshing drink.

ice
1 shot espresso
1 oz. chocolate syrup
2 oz. crème de menthe syrup
1 oz. crème de cacao syrup
cold milk

Fill a 12-ounce glass with ice, add espresso and syrups and fill with cold milk. Stir to combine flavors and serve immediately.

Ginger Pear Iced Mocha Latte

Servings: 1

Ginger, pear and chocolate complement each other well. You can use peach syrup instead of pear in this drink, if you wish.

ice
1 shot espresso
1 oz. chocolate syrup
2 oz. pear syrup
1 oz. ginger syrup
cold milk

Fill a 12-ounce glass with ice, add espresso and syrups and fill with cold milk. Stir to combine flavors and serve immediately.

Fruity Iced Latte

Use one or more of your favorite fruit-flavored syrups for this refreshing drink. Yummy choices include: banana, peach, raspberry, guava and passion fruit.

ice
1 shot espresso
3 oz. fruit-flavored syrup
cold milk

Fill a 12-ounce glass with ice, add espresso and syrup and fill with cold milk. Stir to combine flavors and serve immediately.

Tropical Breeze Iced Latte

Servings: 1

Passion fruit may or may not have aphrodisiac properties, but it is really named for part of the plant's resemblance to the thorns in the crown worn by Christ during his crucifixion. For a variation, add 1 oz. of any tropical-flavored fruit syrup, such as pineapple, coconut or guava.

ice
1 shot espresso
2 oz. banana syrup
1 oz. passion fruit syrup
cold milk

Fill a 12-ounce glass with ice, add espresso and syrups and fill with cold milk. Stir to combine flavors and serve immediately.

Red Cactus Iced Latte

Servings: 1

We found the formula for this drink at a little espresso stand in Arizona. Add a bit of rum or vodka to this latte if desired.

ice
1 shot espresso
2 oz. raspberry syrup
1 oz. kiwi syrup
1 oz. lime syrup
cold milk

Fill a 12-ounce glass with ice, add espresso and syrups and fill with cold milk. Stir to combine flavors and serve immediately.

Iced Mai Tai Latte

Servings: 1

What is better than a taste of the tropics on a hot day? For a real indulgence, substitute rum for rum syrup. Orgeat syrup is a version of almond syrup.

ice
1 shot espresso
1 oz. rum syrup
1 oz. orgeat or almond syrup
1 oz. orange syrup
1 tbs. grenadine
1 tsp. lime juice
cold milk

Fill a 12-ounce glass with ice and add espresso, syrups, grenadine and lime juice. Fill glass with cold milk. Stir to combine flavors and serve immediately.

Iced Raspberry Guava Latte

Guavas are one of our favorite fruits. They are exceptionally high in vitamins and can be served in a variety of ways. At your next brunch, try adding guava syrup or juice to champagne for a refreshing drink.

ice
1 shot espresso
2 oz. raspberry syrup
1 oz. guava syrup
cold milk

Fill a 12-ounce glass with ice, add espresso and syrups and fill with cold milk. Stir to combine flavors and serve immediately.

Iced Melba Latte

This one is a take-off from the popular dessert, Peach Melba.

ice
1 shot espresso
2 oz. peach syrup
1 oz. raspberry syrup
cold milk

Fill a 12-ounce glass with ice, add espresso and syrups and fill with cold milk. Stir to combine flavors and serve immediately.

Trade Winds Iced Latte

Servings: 1

This unusually flavored iced drink is made with tamarind syrup. Some people think it tastes like dates with a touch of lemon or apricot. Tamarinds are the fruit pods of a tropical tree. Their spicy pulp is also used in chutneys and curries.

ice
1 shot espresso
2 oz. tamarind syrup
1 tbs. lemon syrup
cold milk

Fill a 12-ounce glass with ice, add espresso and syrups and fill with cold milk. Stir to combine flavors and serve immediately.

Holiday and Special Occasion Beverages

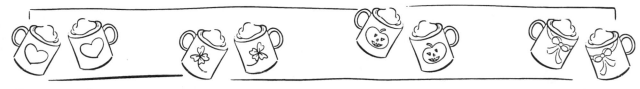

Sweetheart's Cappuccino

Share one of these delightful chocolate-cherry cappuccinos with your sweetheart this February 14th.

1 oz. cherry syrup
1 oz. chocolate syrup
2 shots espresso
steamed and foamed milk

In a 12-ounce cup, combine syrups and espresso. Fill cup with steamed milk and top with foamed milk. Serve immediately.

Anniversary Cappuccino

Servings: 1

Woo your honey all over again with this special drink.

1 oz. raspberry syrup
½ oz. almond or amaretto syrup
1 oz. chocolate fudge syrup
2 shots espresso
steamed and foamed half-and-half
whipped cream
cocoa powder for garnish

In a 12-ounce cup, combine syrups and espresso. Fill cup with steamed half-and-half and top with foamed half-and-half. Top with whipped cream and sprinkle with cocoa.

St. Patrick's Day Mocha

Servings: 1

Top this Shamrock special with whipped cream that has been tinted green with a dash of food coloring. For a real party, use crème de menthe or irish cream liqueur instead of syrup.

1 oz. chocolate or chocolate mint syrup
1 oz. crème de menthe or Irish cream syrup
1 shot espresso
steamed milk
whipped cream, tinted pale green

In an 8-ounce cup, combine syrups and espresso. Fill cup with steamed milk and top with tinted whipped cream.

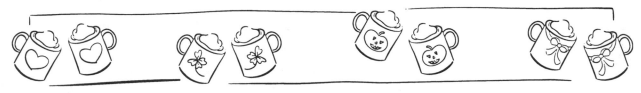

Easter Egg Cappuccino

Servings: 1

This rich cappuccino is reminiscent of those wonderful chocolate eggs that are found in Easter baskets.

1 oz. chocolate fudge syrup
1 oz. grand orange syrup
2 shots espresso
steamed and foamed milk

In a 12-ounce cup, combine syrups and espresso. Fill cup with steamed milk and top with foamed milk. Serve immediately.

Mother's Day Cappuccino

What mother wouldn't enjoy this fruity drink on her special day?

1½ oz. strawberry syrup
½ oz. vanilla syrup
2 shots espresso
steamed and foamed half-and-half
vanilla powder for garnish
1 whole fresh strawberry for garnish

In a 12-ounce cup, combine syrups and espresso. Fill cup with steamed half-and-half, top with foamed half-and-half and sprinkle with vanilla powder. Garnish with strawberry. Serve immediately.

Father's Day Iced Latte

Servings: 1

On his special day, put Dad in his favorite easy chair and bring him one of these cool refreshers.

ice
1 shot espresso
1 oz. chocolate syrup
1 oz. peppermint syrup
cold milk
peppermint candy stick for garnish

Fill a 16-ounce glass with ice, add espresso and syrups and fill with cold milk. Stir to combine flavors, garnish with a peppermint stick and serve immediately.

Witch's Brew

When the neighborhood goblins have finished their tricks this Halloween, relax with one of these.

1 oz. chocolate syrup
1 oz. orange syrup
1 shot espresso
steamed milk
Orange Whipped Cream, page 26
cocoa powder for garnish

In a 12-ounce cup, combine syrups and espresso. Fill cup with steamed milk, top with *Orange Whipped Cream* and sprinkle with cocoa. Serve immediately.

Thanksgiving Latte

Enjoying this latte with loved ones is something to be thankful for!

1 oz. apple syrup
½ oz. cinnamon syrup
2 tsp. honey
1 shot espresso
steamed milk
whipped cream
ground cinnamon for garnish
cinnamon stick for garnish

In an 8-ounce cup, combine syrups, honey and espresso. Fill cup with steamed milk and top with whipped cream. Sprinkle with cinnamon and garnish with cinnamon stick. Serve immediately.

Holiday Eggnog Latte

Commercially prepared eggnog is wonderful steamed and served as a latte. It thickens as it stands, so prepare only enough for one latte at a time. There are many possible variations for this latte. For example, add 1 oz. Swedish rum syrup; add 1 oz. liquor of choice, such as brandy, rum or whisky; add 1 oz. liqueur of choice, such as crème de cacao, Kahlua or Frangelico. Or, add ½ oz. fruit-flavored syrup, such as apricot or peach.

1 shot espresso
5 oz. eggnog, steamed and foamed
nutmeg for garnish

Pour espresso into an 8-ounce cup. Add steamed eggnog, top with foamed eggnog and sprinkle with nutmeg. Serve immediately.

Mocha Eggnog Latte

Offer this concoction after an evening of caroling.

1 oz. chocolate syrup
1 shot espresso
5 oz. eggnog, steamed
whipped cream
nutmeg for garnish

In an 8-ounce cup, combine syrup and espresso. Fill cup with steamed eggnog, top with whipped cream and sprinkle with nutmeg. Serve immediately.

Mardi Gras Punch

Servings: 12

Careful — this punch is smooth, but it packs a whollop!

1 qt. bourbon
6 cups brewed espresso
1 pt. half-and-half
1 cup amaretto
1 qt. vanilla, chocolate or coffee ice cream, softened

In a large bowl or pitcher, combine bourbon, espresso, half-and-half and amaretto. Chill until serving time. To serve, pour mixture into a large punch bowl and spoon in softened ice cream. Ladle into punch cups.

Amaretto Café for a Crowd

Servings: 4

This is a wonderful drink to sip by the fire after a day on the slopes.

2 oz. semisweet chocolate, finely
   chopped
2 oz. unsweetened chocolate, finely
   chopped
⅓ cup granulated sugar
3 tbs. brown sugar

2 cups half-and-half
1 cup amaretto
4 shots espresso
steamed milk
1 cup whipped cream
2 tbs. grated semisweet chocolate

In a heavy saucepan, combine finely chopped chocolates, sugars and half-and-half. Simmer over low heat until chocolate is melted and sugar is dissolved. Cool. Add amaretto and refrigerate until serving time.

To serve, pour ¼ of the mixture into each coffee cup. Add 1 shot espresso to each cup and fill with steamed milk. Top with whipped cream and chocolate shavings. Serve immediately.

Millionaire's Mocha

This is rich, but it's worth splurging on for special occasions. For an extra-special treat, add 1 shot Bailey's Irish Cream, Grand Marnier, amaretto, Kahlua, Galliano, brandy or Southern Comfort to each serving.

4 oz. German's sweet chocolate, chopped
1 can (14 oz.) sweetened condensed milk
1 cup heavy cream, whipped
4 cups hot espresso

In the top of a double boiler, melt chocolate with condensed milk over simmering water until smooth. Cool. Fold in whipped cream and refrigerate until serving time.

To serve, place 1/4 of the mixture in each cup and fill with espresso. Serve immediately.

Espresso Drinks with Spirit

The Great Escape

To get away from it all, sip one of these. If you want the warmth of this drink to last, pour the Bailey's in the mug and heat in the microwave for 20 seconds on MEDIUM before adding the rest of the ingredients.

3 shots Bailey's Irish Cream, warmed if desired
2 shots vodka
1 shot amaretto
1 shot espresso

Combine all ingredients in a coffee mug. Serve immediately.

French Royale Blended Iced Latte

Servings: 1

This delicious cold drink is made with Chambord liqueur. Chambord was first produced in France during the time of King Louis XIV and is made from small black raspberries, other selected fruits and honey.

1 oz. Chambord
1 oz. espresso
1 oz. heavy cream
½ cup crushed ice

In a blender container, combine Chambord, espresso, cream and crushed ice. Mix on high speed for about 25 seconds. Pour into a large cocktail glass and serve immediately.

Café Viennese

*Coffee and chocolate is a classic flavor combination that will always be popular. For an extra special touch, top with **Kahlua-Chocolate Whipped Cream**, page 25.*

1 oz. Kahlua
1 oz. crème de cacao
2 oz. espresso
4 oz. hot water
sweetened whipped cream

In a 10- to 12-ounce mug, combine Kahlua and crème de cacao. Add espresso and hot water and top with sweetened whipped cream. Serve immediately.

Chocolate Café Viennese

Servings: 1

If you are a real chocoholic, try this version of Café Viennese.

1 oz. Kahlua
1 oz. crème de cacao
2 oz. espresso
4 oz. hot chocolate
sweetened whipped cream
shaved chocolate for garnish

In a 10- or 12-ounce mug, combine Kahlua and crème de cacao. Add espresso and hot chocolate and top with sweetened whipped cream and shaved chocolate. Serve immediately.

Café Bavarian

Those of you who like the flavored international coffee mixes will enjoy this.

½ oz. peppermint schnapps
1 oz. Kahlua
2 oz. espresso
4 oz. hot water
sweetened whipped cream

In a 10- to 12-ounce mug, combine peppermint schnapps and Kahlua. Add espresso and hot water and top with sweetened whipped cream. Serve immediately.

Café Caribbean

Servings: 1

If you want to add a touch of elegance, prepare the coffee mugs by moistening the rims with lemon juice and dipping them in granulated sugar.

1 oz. dark rum
1 oz. Tia Maria
2 oz. espresso
4 oz. hot water
sweetened whipped cream or *Kahlua-Chocolate Whipped Cream*, page 25

In an 8- to 12-ounce mug, combine rum and Tia Maria. Add espresso and hot water and top with sweetened whipped cream. Serve immediately.

Café Amaretto

Put your feet up in front of a cozy fire and relax with one of these.

1 oz. amaretto
2 oz. espresso
4 oz. hot water
2 tbs. (heaping) coffee ice cream, softened
ground allspice for garnish

Pour amaretto into an 8- to 12-ounce mug. Add espresso and hot water and top with softened coffee ice cream. Sprinkle with allspice and serve immediately.

Cappuccino Supreme

Vary the liqueur in this drink to suit your taste. Amaretto, Galliano, Frangelico and Kahlua are all delightful.

1 shot espresso
1 oz. amaretto
1 oz. brandy
steamed and foamed milk

In an 8-ounce cup, combine espresso, amaretto and brandy. Fill cup with steamed milk and top with foamed milk. Serve immediately.

West Indies Trade Wind

Servings: 1

We tried a variation of this drink when on vacation in the Caribbean and loved it. Christie favors Meyer's Rum.

1 oz. dark rum
1 oz. amaretto
2 oz. espresso
4 oz. hot water
sweetened whipped cream
cherry for garnish, optional

In a 10-ounce cup or mug, combine rum and amaretto. Add espresso and hot water and top with sweetened whipped cream. Garnish with a cherry if desired. Serve immediately.

The Irish Mountie

Servings: 1

If Dudley Do-right were a drinking man, I imagine he would go for one of these. It's sure to keep anyone warm and awake during cold winter evenings.

1 oz. Yukon Jack
1 oz. Bailey's Irish Cream
2 oz. espresso
4 oz. hot water
sweetened whipped cream

In a 10- to 12-ounce mug, combine Yukon Jack and Bailey's. Add espresso and hot water and top with sweetened whipped cream. Serve immediately.

Café Brûlot

Café Brûlot hails from the bayous of Louisiana. The preparation is fun and will provide some entertainment for your guests. The final preparation should be in a darkened room for the best effect. Hint: Keep the espresso in a thermal carafe until ready to use.

1 small orange
10 whole cloves
1 large orange
1 large lemon
2 cinnamon sticks
5 sugar cubes
½ cup brandy
¼ cup Cointreau
16 oz. hot espresso

Have ready a deep, elegant heatproof bowl, a serving tray and demitasse cups suitable for serving guests. Stud orange with whole cloves and set aside. Next, use a zester to remove outer layer of orange and lemon and place combined zest in the deep bowl along with cinnamon sticks and sugar cubes. Heat ½ cup brandy in a small saucepan, but do not let it boil. When heated, pour brandy over ingredients in bowl. Place bowl on a tray and bring studded orange, bowl and tray, a large ladle, Cointreau and espresso to the serving table.

Carefully ignite brandy mixture and ladle over spices until sugar melts. Pour espresso into bowl. Fill ladle with ¼ cup Cointreau. Carefully place orange in ladle, ignite liqueur, and carefully lower ladle into Café Brûlot, allowing orange to float on the surface. Ladle Café Brûlot into demitasse cups and serve to your guests, who no doubt will be suitably impressed.

Café Parisian

Servings: 1

This recipe, another classic flavor combination, combines espresso, Grand Marnier and brandy. It's an interesting hot drink for a tranquil moment in your life.

1 oz. brandy
1 oz. Grand Marnier
2 oz. espresso
4 oz. hot water
sweetened whipped cream
grated orange peel (zest) for garnish

In a 10- to 12-ounce mug, combine brandy and Grand Marnier. Add espresso and hot water and top with sweetened whipped cream. Garnish with orange peel and serve immediately.

The Mexican Standoff

Servings: 1

Share one of these with your favorite señor or señorita.

1 oz. tequila
1 oz. Kahlua
1 oz. espresso
1 oz. hot water
sweetened whipped cream
cocoa powder for garnish

In a 10- to 12-ounce mug, combine tequila and Kahlua. Add espresso and hot water and top with sweetened whipped cream. Sprinkle with cocoa powder and serve immediately.

Espresso Nudge

This is the espresso version of the familiar Coffee Nudge.

1 oz. brandy
1 oz. crème de cacao liqueur
2 oz. espresso
4 oz. hot water
sweetened whipped cream

In a 10- to 12-ounce mug, combine brandy and crème de cacao. Add espresso and hot water and top with sweetened whipped cream. Serve immediately.

Irish Espresso

St. Patrick himself would like one of these. It's like an Irish coffee using espresso instead of drip-brewed coffee.

1 oz. Irish whiskey
1 oz. Bailey's Irish Cream
2 oz. espresso
4 oz. hot water
2 tsp. turbinado sugar
sweetened whipped cream

In a 10- to 12-ounce mug, combine Irish whiskey and Bailey's Irish Cream. Add espresso and hot water. Add turbinado sugar and stir until dissolved. Top with sweetened whipped cream and serve immediately.

Rocky Road Mocha

Servings: 1

Frangelico is a popular liqueur with the taste of toasted hazelnuts.

1 oz. Frangelico
1 oz. crème de cacao
2 oz. espresso
4 oz. hot chocolate
miniature marshmallows

In a 10- to 12-ounce mug, combine Frangelico, crème de cacao, espresso and hot chocolate. Top with miniature marshmallows and serve immediately.

Cherry Rum Heater

Save money on your utility bill and turn up the heat with this instead.

1 oz. cherry-flavored brandy
1 oz. light rum
2 oz. espresso
4 oz. hot water
sweetened whipped cream
stemmed cherry for garnish

In a 10- to 12-ounce mug, combine brandy and rum. Add espresso and hot water and top with sweetened whipped cream. Garnish with cherry and serve immediately.

Restless in Renton

Servings: 1

After seeing the popular movie, "Sleepless in Seattle," we decided to name a coffee drink after our town, thus, "Restless in Renton." Although we must confess, after one of these we go right to sleep.

2 oz. Kahlua
2 oz. brandy
1 shot espresso
5 oz. half-and-half, steamed
sweetened whipped cream

In a 10- to 12-ounce mug, combine Kahlua, brandy, espresso and steamed half-and-half. Top with whipped cream and serve immediately.

New Orleans Cooler

Drink this one quickly and join the Mardi Gras parade!

1 oz. bourbon
1 oz. praline syrup
2 oz. espresso
6-8 oz. cold milk
½ cup crushed ice

In a cocktail shaker, combine bourbon, praline syrup, espresso, milk and ice and shake well. Strain into a 12-ounce tumbler and serve immediately.

Cabo Cooler

Servings: 1

We visited Cabo San Lucas a few years ago where we were served a variation of this in the hotel lounge. I don't recall what they called it, but Cabo Cooler seems appropriate.

1 oz. Kahlua
1 oz. dark rum
4 oz. espresso
2 oz. heavy cream
1 tsp. sugar
½ cup crushed ice

In a cocktail shaker, combine Kahlua, rum, espresso, cream, sugar and ice and shake well. Strain into a 12-ounce tumbler and serve immediately.

White Russian

Vodka gives this icy drink its Russian flair.

1 oz. Kahlua
1 oz. vodka
4 oz. chilled espresso
4 oz. half-and-half
½ cup crushed ice
sugar to taste

In a cocktail shaker, combine Kahlua, vodka, espresso, half-and-half and ice and shake well. Taste and add sugar. Strain into a 12-ounce tumbler and serve immediately.

Jamaica Joy Soda

Servings: 1

Add a bit of joy to your evening.

1 oz. dark rum
4 oz. espresso
4 oz. half-and-half
soda water
sugar to taste

In a bowl or pitcher, combine rum, espresso and half-and-half and chill until cold. Pour into a tall glass filled with ice and top with soda water. Add sugar to taste. Stir with a long spoon or a straw to combine flavors and serve immediately.

The Velvet Hammer

Watch out: This drink is smooth, but too many will nail you in the end.

1 oz. vodka
1 oz. crème de cacao
2 oz. espresso
6 oz. half-and-half
½ cup crushed ice
sugar to taste

In a cocktail shaker, combine vodka, crème de cacao, espresso, half-and-half and ice and shake well. Strain into a tall glass and add sugar. Serve immediately.

Grasshopper Cooler

Servings: 1

Smooth and so refreshing!

1 oz. vodka
1 oz. white crème de menthe
1 oz. white crème de cacao
4 oz. espresso, chilled
1 oz. half-and-half
½ cup crushed ice

In a blender container, combine vodka, crème de menthe, crème de cacao, espresso, half-and-half and crushed ice and blend until smooth. Pour into a chilled tall glass and serve immediately.

Something Different: Frappes, Shakes and Floats

Mocha Frappe

On a hot summer day, this one will cool you down and wake you up.

ice
1 shot espresso
3 oz. coffee syrup
2 oz. half-and-half

Fill a blender container half full of ice. Add espresso, syrup and half-and-half. Blend until smooth and pour into a tall serving glass.

Hawaiian Paradise Frappe

Using coconut cream in this drink gives it richness.

ice
1 shot espresso
2 tbs. coconut cream or coconut syrup
1 oz. chocolate syrup
1 oz. macadamia nut syrup
2 oz. half-and-half

Fill a blender container half full of ice. Add espresso, cream of coconut, syrups and half-and-half. Blend until smooth and pour into a tall serving glass.

The Vagabond

For centuries coconuts have provided essential nutrients. Explorers used their meat for nourishment and their liquid for survival.

ice
1 shot espresso
2 tbs. cream of coconut
2 oz. pineapple syrup
1 oz. rum syrup or rum
2 oz. half-and-half

Fill a blender container half full of ice. Add espresso, cream of coconut, syrups and half-and-half. Blend until smooth and pour into a tall serving glass.

Razzle Dazzle Frappe

This smooth, cold drink is loaded with flavor and color.

ice
1 shot espresso
1 oz. raspberry syrup
½ oz. almond syrup
2 oz. half-and-half

Fill a blender container half full of ice. Add espresso, syrups and half-and-half. Blend until smooth and pour into a tall serving glass.

Sunrise Smoothie

Servings: 1

Whenever your bananas get too ripe, just throw them in the freezer, skins and all. To use, thaw briefly and peel. Cut bananas into 1-inch chunks while still frozen. Frozen bananas add delicious flavor and texture to frappes and shakes.

ice
1 shot espresso
1 banana, frozen, peeled and cut into chunks
1 oz. vanilla syrup
2 oz. half-and-half

Fill a blender container half full of ice. Add espresso, banana chunks, syrup and half-and-half. Blend until smooth and pour into a tall serving glass.

Coffee Shake

The cold temperature and blend of coffee flavors will perk you up when you are feeling the heat.

2 oz. Kahlua syrup or coffee syrup
1 shot espresso
1 cup milk
1 scoop coffee ice cream

In a blender container, combine Kahlua syrup, espresso, milk and ice cream. Blend until smooth and pour into a tall serving glass.

Espresso Eggnog Shake

This frothy drink is a rich treat during the holiday season.

1 shot espresso
2 oz. Swedish rum syrup
1 cup purchased eggnog
1 scoop eggnog ice cream or vanilla ice cream

In a blender container, combine espresso, syrup, eggnog and ice cream. Blend until smooth and pour into a tall serving glass.

Banana Fudge Shake

Servings: 1

Use a frozen banana to give this shake a thick, foamy consistency.

1 shot espresso
1 banana, frozen, peeled and cut into chunks
1 oz. banana syrup
1 oz. chocolate syrup
½ oz. vanilla syrup
1 cup milk
1 scoop chocolate ice cream

In a blender container, combine espresso, banana chunks, syrups, milk and ice cream. Blend until smooth and pour into a tall serving glass.

Frosty the Snowman

Peppermint delivers a burst of icy fresh flavor. If your shakes are too thick, add more milk.

1 shot espresso
2 oz. peppermint syrup
1 cup milk
1 scoop peppermint ice cream

In a blender container, combine espresso, syrup, milk and ice cream. Blend until smooth and pour into a tall serving glass.

Black Cherry Shake

Use vanilla, chocolate or cherry ice cream for this sweet shake.

1 shot espresso
2 oz. cherry syrup
1 oz. chocolate syrup
1 cup milk
1 scoop vanilla ice cream

In a blender container, combine espresso, syrups, milk and ice cream. Blend until smooth and pour into a tall serving glass.

Neapolitan Shake

This is inspired by the rectangular-shaped packages of three-flavored ice creams popular with children. You can use a food processor, in addition to a blender, to make shakes.

1 shot espresso
1 oz. chocolate syrup
1 oz. strawberry syrup
1 oz. vanilla syrup
1 cup cold milk
1 scoop vanilla ice cream

In a blender container, combine espresso, syrups, milk and ice cream. Blend until smooth and pour into a tall serving glass.

Kona Coffee Float

Slip on your headphones, put in your favorite CD and sip this delicious drink — bliss. You can also serve this as a hot drink topped with whipped cream.

1 cup espresso, chilled
1 oz. Tia Maria
2 oz. brandy
1 tbs. brown sugar
1 small scoop vanilla ice cream

In a tall serving glass, stir together espresso, Tia Maria, brandy and sugar until sugar dissolves. Top with ice cream.

Banana Cow Float

Banana syrup gives this drink a rich and satisfying old-fashioned flavor.

1 shot espresso
1 oz. banana syrup
1 oz. chocolate syrup
½ oz. vanilla syrup
6 oz. soda water
1 scoop vanilla or chocolate ice cream

In a tall milkshake glass, combine espresso and syrups. Stir well with a long spoon. Fill glass with soda water and top with ice cream.

Espresso Ice Cream Cooler

Servings: 1

A popular license plate frame in Seattle states: "Powered by Espresso."

1 cup cold milk
1 shot espresso
1 oz. French vanilla syrup
1 scoop vanilla ice cream
whipped cream
shaved chocolate for garnish

In a tall serving glass, combine milk, espresso and syrup. Top with ice cream and whipped cream and garnish with shaved chocolate.

Cherries Jubilee Float

Servings: 1

Have this soda for dessert!

1 shot espresso
2 oz. Bing cherry syrup
½ oz. rum syrup
6 oz. soda water
1 scoop cherry ice cream or vanilla ice cream

In a tall serving glass, combine espresso and syrups and stir well. Fill glass with soda water and top with ice cream.

Espresso Chocolate Chip Mint Float

Here's a great way to use one of America's favorite ice cream flavors.

1 shot espresso
2 oz. chocolate mint syrup
1 oz. chocolate ice cream topping
6 oz. soda water
1 scoop chocolate chip mint ice cream

In a tall serving glass, combine espresso, syrup and topping and stir well. Fill glass with soda water and top with ice cream.

Steamers

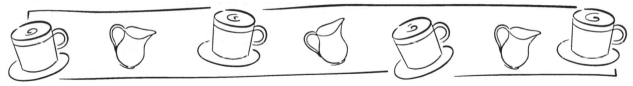

Almond Moo Steamer

This is one of our favorite bedtime soothers.

2 oz. almond syrup
steamed milk

Pour syrup into an 8-ounce cup and fill with steamed milk.

Chocolate Steamer

Drinking chocolate beverages began with the Aztecs. For variations, try choco-late fudge, chocolate malt or chocolate mint syrup.

2 oz. chocolate syrup
steamed milk

Pour syrup into an 8-ounce cup and fill with steamed milk.

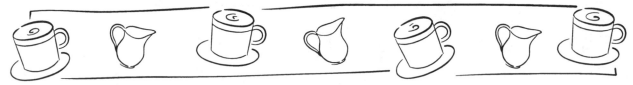

Chocolate Velvet Steamer

Servings: 1

Chocolate has always been associated with passion.

1 oz. chocolate syrup
1 oz. rum syrup
steamed milk

Combine syrups in a 8-ounce cup and fill cup with steamed milk.

Hot Nutty Irish Steamer

Servings: 1

You'll go nuts over this combination!

1 oz. Irish cream syrup
1 oz. hazelnut syrup
steamed milk

Combine syrups in an 8-ounce cup and fill cup with steamed milk.

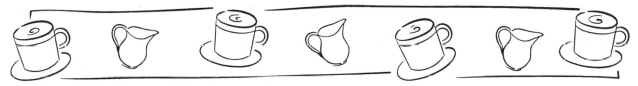

Almond Apricot Steamer

Servings: 1

Apricot and almond flavors complement each other in many delicious foods. Most of the apricots grown in the United States come from the San Joaquin Valley in California. You can substitute peach, raspberry, cherry or strawberry syrup for apricot if you wish.

1 oz. almond syrup
1 oz. apricot syrup
steamed milk

Combine syrups in an 8-ounce cup and fill cup with steamed milk.

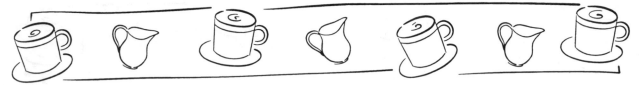

Peppermint Steamer

You will be off to the land of sweet dreams after you've sipped one of these.

2 oz. peppermint or crème de menthe syrup
steamed milk

Pour syrup into an 8-ounce cup and fill cup with steamed milk.

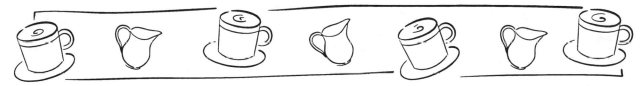

Apple Cobbler Steamer

It seems strange to see signs on Chinese restaurants in Seattle: "Espresso Served Here."

1 oz. apple syrup
½ oz. walnut syrup
steamed milk
cinnamon for garnish

Combine syrups in an 8-ounce cup and fill with steamed milk. Sprinkle with cinnamon.

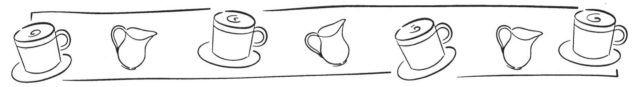

Snow Cap Steamer

Seattle is "Latte Land." One popular bumper sticker warns: "Caution — I brake for lattes." Make delicious variations of this by substituting caramel, butterscotch or macadamia nut syrup for vanilla.

2 oz. vanilla syrup
steamed milk

Pour syrup into an 8-ounce cup and fill with steamed milk.

INDEX